# Low Cost/No Cost Tips for Sustainability in Cultural Heritage

# Low Cost/No Cost Tips for Sustainability in Cultural Heritage

Reduce Your Impact
on the Planet

**Lorraine Finch**

Copyright © 2022 Lorraine Finch

The author has made every effort to ensure the accuracy of the information within this book. The author does not assume and hereby disclaims any liability to any party for any loss, damage, or disruption caused by errors or omissions, whether such errors or omissions result from accident, negligence, or any other cause.

All rights reserved.

No part of this publication may be reproduced, stored in a retrieval system, or transmitted, in any form or by any means, without the prior permission in writing of the author.

FIRST EDITION

www.lfcp.co.uk

978-1-80227-440-0: eBook
978-1-80227-441-7: paperback

# Contents

Welcome . . . . . . . . . . . . . . . . . . . . . . . . . . . . . . . . . . 1
Let's get started . . . . . . . . . . . . . . . . . . . . . . . . . . . . . 3
    *Blockers* . . . . . . . . . . . . . . . . . . . . . . . . . . . . . . . . . . 4
    *The Four Rs* . . . . . . . . . . . . . . . . . . . . . . . . . . . . . . . 5
    *Your actions count* . . . . . . . . . . . . . . . . . . . . . . . . . . 5
    *Carbon Jargon* . . . . . . . . . . . . . . . . . . . . . . . . . . . . . 6

**1**  Equipment and Materials . . . . . . . . . . . . . . . . . . . . 9
**2**  Energy. . . . . . . . . . . . . . . . . . . . . . . . . . . . . . . . . . . 21
**3**  Water . . . . . . . . . . . . . . . . . . . . . . . . . . . . . . . . . . . 27
**4**  In your studio . . . the collection, your office and the kitchen. . . 31
    *In your studio and the collection* . . . . . . . . . . . . . . . 32
    *In the office* . . . . . . . . . . . . . . . . . . . . . . . . . . . . . . 37
    *In the kitchen*. . . . . . . . . . . . . . . . . . . . . . . . . . . . . 40
    *From the archive*. . . . . . . . . . . . . . . . . . . . . . . . . . . 41

**5**  Digital. . . . . . . . . . . . . . . . . . . . . . . . . . . . . . . . . . 45
**6**  Travel and Transport . . . . . . . . . . . . . . . . . . . . . . . 53

| | | |
|---|---|---|
| **7** | Money.................................................. | .59 |
| **8** | Inspiring others/Influencing stakeholders/<br>Changing behaviour ............................. | .65 |
| **9** | Recycling............................................... | .71 |
| **10** | Think .................................................. | .77 |
| | Let's wrap up . . . ................................... | .81 |
| | Notes .................................................. | .85 |
| | References............................................. | .91 |
| | *Books*................................................. | .91 |
| | *Articles*............................................... | .91 |
| | *Videos*................................................ | .92 |
| | About the author.................................... | .93 |

24.2.22

Dear Lorraine Finch,

Thank you for all you are doing to help in the fight against climate change.

Best wishes

David Attenborough

*from David Attenborough*

Letter from Sir David Attenborough

# Welcome

Welcome to my tips for low cost/no cost actions to reduce your impact on the climate and the environment. As well as reducing your impact, implementing some or all of these tips will also have a positive effect on your wellbeing and the wellbeing of others.

I was moved to make these tips available because so many times I have heard from others that they felt powerless to effect change, that the actions they needed to take were too costly and that the steps needed took too long to have an impact.

Read on and discover:

- Actions that *are* in your power to take straight away for little or no cost which will have an immediate and positive effect on the climate and the environment.

# Let's get started . . .

This guide is intended for all who work in cultural heritage, whether in a museum, library, archive, gallery or any other situation. If you are a curator, conservator, archivist, librarian, front of house, volunteer or fulfilling one of the many other roles in cultural heritage, you will find tips here for you. Many of the tips and actions apply wherever you work, so whether you are a lorry driver, nurse, CEO, astronaut or anything else, keep reading. These tips are equally applicable to the self-employed and the employed. Whether you are working on your own or in an organisation with 100+ colleagues, these tips are for you.

The tips and actions are given in TEN sections:

- Equipment and Materials
- Energy
- Water
- In your studio . . . the collection, your office and the kitchen
- Digital
- Travel and Transport
- Money
- Inspiring others/Influencing stakeholders/Changing behaviour
- Recycling
- Think

You can read them all or dip into the sections which are the most relevant to you.

You can put all of the tips into action or select a few. *Don't worry* if you can't do everything; doing something is better than doing nothing. Don't let the thought that you need to do either everything or nothing stop you from doing something. It's better to take some action than none at all. Start where you can.

'**The way to get started is to quit talking and start doing.**'
**Walt Disney**

## Blockers

We all have blockers to getting started with taking action on the climate and the environment:

- **Fear:** Fear of making the wrong choice. It's important to recognise that sometimes you will get it wrong. You won't always be able to make the best decision. *Don't worry.* Learn and move on. Please tell others what worked and what didn't. That way we can all learn.
- **Guilt:** You might enjoy a steak, live in a draughty C19th house, or fly for work. So what? There are trade-offs we all need to accept. It's time to put the hair shirt aside and let go of your guilt. Do what you can.
- **Going without or giving things up:** Sustainability is not about frugality or doing anything tedious. It's about changing habits. It's about breaking away from our current TAKE, MAKE, WASTE model to REFUSING, REDUCING, REUSING and RECYCLING.

Let's get started . . .

## The Four Rs

**REFUSE**: Think about what you buy and use in your workplace. Refuse to purchase more than you need. Refuse to purchase wasteful products and those which are difficult to recycle. Refuse to support businesses and organisations that damage the climate and the environment.

**REDUCE**: Reduce the amount that you use. Reduce the amount you purchase. Reduce your use of harmful, wasteful products and products that are not easy to recycle. Use the minimum amount required to avoid unnecessary waste.

**REUSE**: Choose reusable options. Avoid single-use items. Reuse items.

**RECYCLE**: At the end of an item's usable life, recycle it.

## Your actions count

> 'Climate change is such a vexed, complex issue that if it is not approached from a perspective that includes everyone, we are not going to get there.'[1]

Each individual action makes a difference. If you feel that switching off the lights or having a vegetarian lunch is not going to make much difference, remember that others are also acting.

'Small changes can make a big difference.'[2] Collective change is created by countless individuals. Here's a great example: internationally, $11 trillion of pension investments have been divested from fossil fuels,[3] partly as a result of pressure from consumers – that's you! Here's another great example: the Natural History Museum (NHM) made a 7% saving on their energy bills by simple steps such as turning off equipment overnight.[4]

> **'Every one of us makes a difference every single day.'**
> **Dr Jane Goodall**[5]

The example of the saving made by the NHM counters the argument that it is not possible to take sustainability actions because they are too costly. The truth is:

- Sustainability actions do not have to cost you and/or your organisation money.
- Sustainability actions will actually save you and/or your organisation money.

'In a single year, Theatre Royal Plymouth saved £10,000 just by changing its water management system; the Sage Gateshead has saved 44% on its electricity per concert by changing light bulbs and air conditioning filters; installing new LED lighting has saved the Royal & Derngate Theatre 60 per cent [sic] on their utility costs.'[6]

**Saving the earth does not cost the earth!**

# Carbon Jargon

Be careful with the terms. Question how they are being used. Think about what they mean in the context in which they are being used.

- Sustainable – is it? What definition of sustainable is being used? Here's something to think about: palm oil is often described as

being sustainable, but virgin tropical rainforest had to be cut down to grow the oil palm trees in the first instance.
- Compostable – is it? Is it home compostable or industrial compostable? If it's industrial compostable, do facilities exist to do this? How long will it take to compost?
- Environmentally friendly – how? More environmentally friendly than what?
- Biodegradable – under what conditions? How long will it take?
- Recyclable – commonly recycled? Most materials are recyclable but can't be recycled because facilities don't exist.
- Better for the environment – better than what?
- Green – and . . .?

# 1 Equipment and Materials

All of the equipment and materials that you use have associated greenhouse gas (GHG) emissions. The main sources are:

- Raw materials
- Manufacture
- Transportation
- Energy used to power the equipment
- Disposal

With regard to transportation, most of us think in terms of the transport from the supplier to us, but what about the shipping? Most of what we use has, at one point, travelled on a container ship. '50,000 merchant ships carry more than 11 billion metric tonnes of cargo annually = 80% of world trade. Every merchant ship runs on fossil fuels.'[7] 'If maritime shipping were a country, it would be the world's sixth largest polluter.'[8]

Globally, trade has increased five to sixfold in the last 50 years. That's twice the population using 5.5x more stuff.[9] Earth Overshoot Day marks the date when our demand for ecological resources and services in a given year exceeds what the planet can regenerate in that year. In 2021, it fell on July 29th!

Think about the equipment and materials that you use. What are they? You might want to create a list. You'll be surprised by the amount you use. Think about not only the equipment and materials you use to care for the heritage but ALL of the equipment and materials that you use, including in your office and the kitchen. In this guide, equipment and materials refers to everything that is used in the workplace, whether that's the HVAC, leafcaster, hand tools, printer, chairs, shelves, mobile phones and so on . . .

## Tips

★ Equipment and tools should be carefully looked after, repaired frequently to maintain energy efficiency, and refurbished (where possible) rather than thrown away. They should be replaced by new only when they have reached the end of their life. Don't ask for new or upgraded equipment unless you really need it.

★ Extend the lifespan of equipment with careful handling and frequent maintenance.

○ Keep operations and maintenance manuals up to date to ensure that equipment is maintained in top condition.

★ Repair equipment rather than replacing it. Equipment you no longer need may still be useful to others. Think how it can be reused, donated, repurposed, recycled or stored. Waste from Electrical and Electronic Equipment (WEEE) recycling schemes can ensure safe disposal. (WEEE estimates that almost a quarter of used electrical products taken to household waste recycling centres each year could be reused, with a gross value of £200 million.[10]

### Equipment and Materials

★ Use equipment that is appropriately sized for the job, e.g. no large fridge if all you have in it is a jar of starch paste.
★ When you replace equipment:

- Make sure that you purchase energy efficient equipment.

    *www.sust-it.net gives details of energy-efficient household electricals including freezers, fridges, desktops, laptops, printers, copiers, light bulbs, heaters and kettles. It also lists the annual running cost.*

- Buy the best quality you can afford to ensure that you can use it for as long as possible.
- Purchase equipment which:

    → is designed to have a long usable life. Avoid equipment that has been designed for premature obsolescence
    → can be repaired. Avoid equipment that is difficult to repair
    → has spare parts readily available long term
    → can be recycled at the end of its life
    → is designed for disassembly (i.e. can be broken down at the end of its life)

AND

    → where the components can be reused
    → where the constituent items are easy to recycle.

Your mantra for equipment should be *Durable, Repairable, Recyclable.*

★ Check whether the manufacturer has a take back scheme for recycling at the end of the usable life of the equipment.
★ Use equipment and materials that have reused components and recycled content, e.g. printing paper or boxes for short-term storage.

# Low Cost/No Cost Tips for Sustainability in Cultural Heritage

- ★ The amount of material that we send for recycling outstrips our demand for products made from them.
- ★ Use what you have. Having equipment and materials unused in a cupboard is a climate cost.
- ★ Use materials fully; e.g. write on both sides of a piece of paper, cut open tubes to use all of the product and reuse waste paper as scrap for notes or to protect surfaces when pasting out.
- ★ Reuse everything.
- ★ Organise. That way you'll know what materials and equipment you have and where they are. This will stop you from buying something and then discovering that you had it already.
- ★ Label materials to ensure that you know what you have and to avoid buying more than you need. It's a good idea to add the purchase date, the date you opened it and the use-by date (if appropriate) because some materials such as Microchamber and pheromone pest traps lose their efficacy in storage.
- ★ Carry out a waste audit to identify what waste you are creating. You could look at the total amount of waste you generate, the types of waste (and amount of each type of waste), what's thrown away, in other words what goes to landfill or incineration, and what waste is recycled. This will help you to work out how you can reduce the waste you produce and how you can reuse and recycle your waste.
- ★ If you need to buy materials and equipment, buy them in one order. This will avoid the need for multiple deliveries and so reduce the GHG emissions associated with deliveries. Aim for one or two orders a year.
- ★ Coordinate orders with others to reduce deliveries even further. Contact your regional Conservation Development Officer (CDO) or Museum Development Officer (MDO). They may be able to organise a group purchase.
- ★ Avoid last-minute, one-off deliveries by early decision making and no late changes of mind.

## Equipment and Materials

★ Buy locally. Deliveries are more sustainable if they're local because this reduces the GHG emissions associated with transport.
★ Buy only the amount you need.
★ Buy in bulk if you know that you will use it all.
★ Buy the right quantity for what is required. If you only need one tube of paste or three sheets of board, then buy only that. Contact your suppliers before purchasing to ask whether this is possible. If it's not possible, ask them why not.

> 'Telling suppliers that ethical or environmental aspects matter to your business sends a clear message that . . . things need to change!'[11]

★ Think about where your equipment and materials have come from. For example, have they been shipped from the other side of the globe? Do they contain conflict minerals? Has rainforest been cut down to grow the raw material? Ask your supplier for information.
★ Contact your suppliers and question them about their actions on sustainability.
★ Contact your supplier and ask whether your order can be delivered via public transport or bicycle courier.
  o If you live near your supplier or pass them on your way to work, ask whether you can pop in to collect your order.

★ Research your suppliers' ethics and environmental practices. 'Ethical Consumer Magazine' rates companies on their "ethiscore" – an assessment of policies and actions towards people, politics, the environment and animals, looking at issues such as workers' rights, fossil fuel investment, and pollution.'[12]
★ Choose suppliers based on their climate strategy and the transparency of their emissions data.

- o It is estimated that 60% of global Gross Domestic Product (GDP) is in the hands of consumers.[13] This gives you tremendous power to create change simply by shifting your spending to accountable and sustainable suppliers.

★ Request that your suppliers commit to the 1.5°C ambition and halve emissions before 2030. Include this in your procurement criteria and your supplier code of conduct.
★ Check out the certifications of both your suppliers and their products. Certifications such as BCorp, Fairtrade, FSC certified paper or Soil Association labels give you an indication of the sustainability of the product and the sustainability ethos of the business.
★ Develop a sustainable purchasing policy. This is a list of your typical purchases, including materials and equipment, with details about what can and cannot be purchased and what you and/or your colleagues should look for, or avoid, when trying to purchase sustainable options.
★ Replace equipment and materials with those that have a smaller environmental cost, such as blotter with Evolon or plastic-containing tea bags with plant-based, biodegradable tea bags.
★ Use fewer hazardous materials.
★ Reduce the amount of new equipment and materials you purchase. Here are some alternatives you can use:

## Alternative sources for equipment and materials:

★ Look out for cultural heritage organisations that are being refurbished.

### Examples:

◆ A museum refurbished and gave away all their office furniture and office supplies. They also gave away surplus display

# Equipment and Materials

cases, exhibition materials and materials from the education department.

- ◆ An archive which moved buildings gave away all the surplus packing materials at the end of the project. This included Plastazote, boxes, boxboard and acid-free tissue.

★ Find schools which are being refurbished. Look out especially for schools which are refurbishing their labs. You'll be able to get hold of benches, glassware, microscopes and much more – even extraction units.

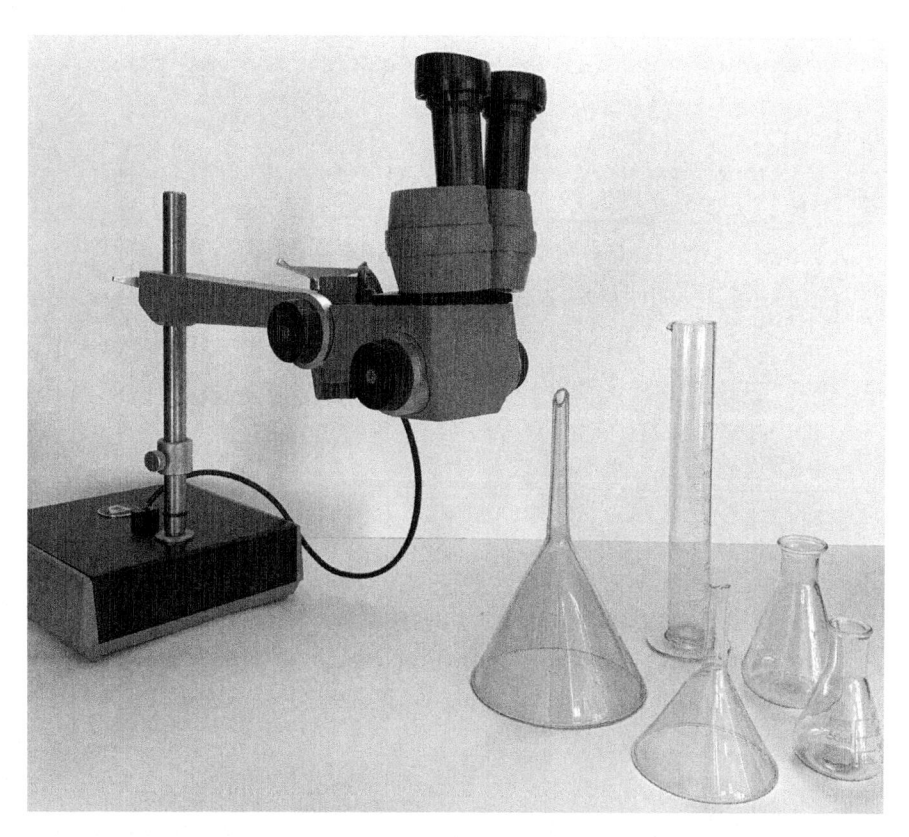

Binocular microscope and glassware sourced from a University laboratory refit

- ★ Keep an eye out for shop refits. They often give away shelving and display units which make excellent workbenches. They may give away mannequins which you could use in the display, and clothing rails which could be used by you or by the public to hang their coats on.
- ★ Ask at your dentist's and hospital. They often have hand tools, furniture and X-ray units (which can be used as light boxes) going spare.
- ★ Do you go to the podiatrist? Ask them for the small scissors and files they no longer use.
- ★ Check out your government's website, e.g. GC Surplus (Canada): They sell surplus federal government assets from furniture to farm equipment, forfeited goods and large-volume materials such as wood and metals. They are a good source for furniture such as plan chests and drawers.

    *https://www.gcsurplus.ca/mn-eng.cfm?snc=wfsav&vndsld=0*

- ★ Contact your conservation/preservation suppliers. Many sell off-cuts, end of rolls, old stock and materials that they have purchased to test. As a result, you may be able to buy in the small quantity that you require. You'll probably find that the suppliers are only too happy to let you take such items for free because they are pleased to clear the space.

### Example:

- ◆ A conservation studio has sourced Tyvek, repair tissue, Bondina, fly mesh, sprayers, weights, a drying rack and brushes for free in this way.

- ★ Ask others. If you need only a small amount, put a call out on your socials. Use your networks.
- ★ Use Museums Freecycle and Freecycle.

## Equipment and Materials

**Example:**

- ◆ A conservator sourced lamps for their work bench, an ultrasonic cleaner and recording equipment using Freecycle.

    *Museums Freecycle: https://www.freecycle.org/town/MuseumUK*
    *Freecycle: https://www.freecycle.org*

★ Have a look at Freegle. They match you with local offers and gives for free.

   *https://www.ilovefreegle.org*

★ Try eBay, Gumtree, Shpock, JiscMail and other online sites for trading used stuff.

   *eBay: https://www.ebay.co.uk*
   *Gumtree: https://www.gumtree.com*
   *Shpock: https://www.shpock.com/en-gb*
   *jiscmail: https://www.jiscmail.ac.uk*

★ Contact your police service. They hold auctions of lost property and seized items. This could be anything from a bike to a MacBook, a power drill or a Dyson vacuum cleaner.
   Check out this guide: 'Police Auctions: How to Legally Buy Stolen Stuff'

   *https://www.moneysavingexpert.com/shopping/police-auctions/*

★ Nip down to your high street and have a look at what's on offer in the second-hand retailers, such as Cash Converters, and the charity shops.

★ Ask for equipment donations from the public and from companies. This is great engagement and demonstrates what you and/or your organisation are doing to help the climate and the environment.

You can include storytelling; e.g. 'We need x to display/conserve/store y which was used by z. Can you help?'.

## *Share and borrow*

- ★ Borrow equipment and loan out yours to others in the sector and to other organisations.
- ★ Have a pool of equipment and materials which you share with other departments.
- ★ Share your surplus materials with others. This could be through your networks or socials and/or by putting it outside with a sign saying 'Free. Please Take'.
- ★ Coordinate your work. If you need specialist equipment for a short period of time, work with another person or organisation to reduce the GHG emissions associated with transporting the equipment to you. It will also reduce the cost to you.

### Example:

- ◆ Two museums had a mould outbreak. They were located close to one another. They coordinated their work and shared the hire of a document cleaning station.

## *Hire*

- ★ Hire. There's a lot of equipment that you can hire. From the conservation suppliers, you can hire a Bassaire document cleaning station, vacuum packer, display cases and the Depulvera book cleaner. From high street electrical stores, you can hire vacuum cleaners, computers, fridges, freezers, microwaves and ovens. You can also lease lighting systems and hire plastic crates and bikes. You can even hire microscopes on a weekly or a monthly basis. Hire a microscope from *www.laboratoryanalysis.co.uk*

# 2 Energy

What energy do you use in the course of your work? It's probably more than you realise, especially when you consider all the areas of your work. Think about all the areas where you use energy. This could include the energy you use for:

- Heating and cooling your workspace
- Lighting
- Heating, ventilation and air conditioning (HVAC) in the exhibition and storage areas
- Energy for equipment such as the suction table, tacking irons, hand drills, office equipment, even the kitchen kettle . . .
- Purchased goods and services such as storage boxes, your laptop, display cases and even your office chair!

Have you heard of SCOPE EMISSIONS? These are really helpful in guiding your thinking about where you are using energy.

Scope emissions are the GHG emissions associated with the running of an organisation or business. Scope emissions are divided into Scope 1, 2 and 3 emissions:

SCOPE 1 – These are direct emissions from owned or controlled sources such as company vehicles and on-site boilers.

SCOPE 2 – These are indirect emissions from the generation of purchased electricity, steam, heating and cooling consumed by your organisation or business. These include the electricity and/or gas for heating, lighting, equipment and environmental control.

SCOPE 3 – All other indirect emissions that occur in your organisation or businesses chain. These include all travel (staff and visitors), waste disposal, and goods and services purchased.

The scope emissions reinforce the fact that everything you do has an impact. So, let's get onto the tips for reducing your energy consumption.

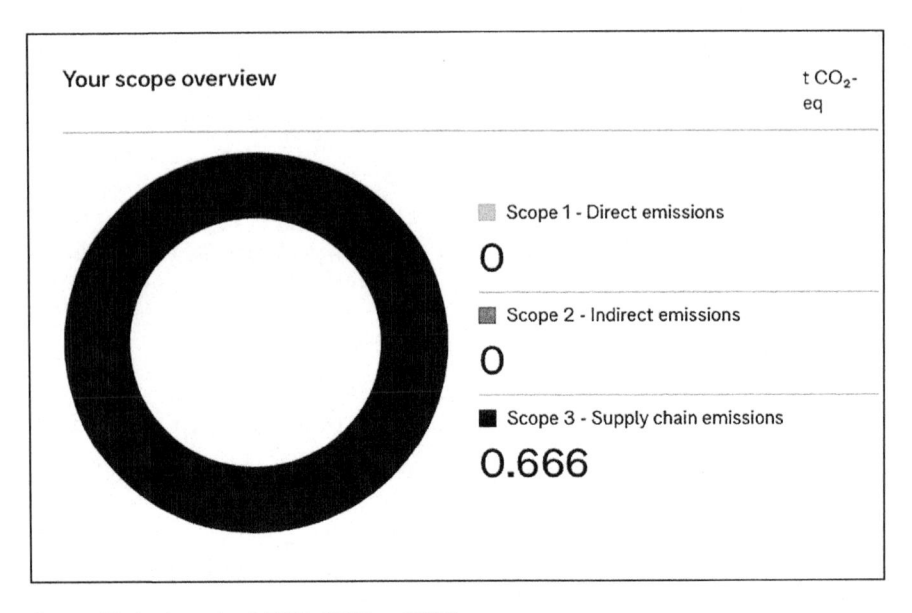

**Your scope overview**  t $CO_2$-eq

Scope 1 - Direct emissions

0

Scope 2 - Indirect emissions

0

Scope 3 - Supply chain emissions

0.666

Scope Emissions for LFCP, 2021 to 2022

Energy

## Tips

★ Switch to a renewable energy supplier.

  o Not all renewable energy suppliers are created equal. Check out 'Green Energy Tariffs for Businesses'. A handy guide on how to choose a renewable energy supplier and how to spot a 'bad' supplier.

  *https://bristolgreencapital.org/spotlight-on-green-energy-tariffs-for-businesses/*

★ Use natural lighting. Rearrange your workspace to allow you to take advantage of natural light.
★ Clean the windows both inside and out. Dirty windows can reduce light levels by 50%!
★ Clean light fittings. Dirt on light fittings can reduce light output by 30%.
★ Switch off lights when they're not in use. If the room will be unoccupied for more than 5 minutes, switch off the lights when you leave.

  'A single light left on overnight over a year accounts for as much greenhouse gas as driving from Cambridge to Paris!'[14]

  'Turning off unneeded lights could remove 171 kg (376 lb) of CO2 emissions per year.'[15]

★ Switch off and unplug equipment when it's not in use. Some equipment continues to consume energy when switched off but still plugged in. You'll see this referred to as 'energy leakage', 'phantom energy' or 'energy vampires'. You can check which pieces of equipment are doing this by using a meter monitor.
★ Put up 'Switch Off' signs.

- ★ Label the switches, so you know which switch controls which light (and which piece of equipment).
- ★ Set up a 'last one out' plan. That is, the last person to leave checks that all the lights and equipment are switched off and unplugged. You could assign this role to a specific member of staff. You could appoint a SWITCH OFF TSAR or a SWITCH MONITOR. Have *FUN*.

   *'Office lights left on overnight consume almost enough energy to heat a home for five months.'*[16]

- ★ Do work in batches. Switching equipment on and off uses more energy if the equipment has to power up each time before it can be used.
- ★ Reduce the amount of time that exhibitions are open to visitors. This will reduce the energy used for lighting, and maybe even the energy used for heating and environmental control.
   - o This might not be very popular with your visitors so put up signs explaining that you are doing this to reduce your GHG emissions. Most of your visitors will understand and applaud your sustainability actions. PLUS it's great communication of your sustainability efforts.
- ★ Reduce light levels in the exhibition areas, the stores and the workspaces.
- ★ Shut down your HVAC for short periods, e.g. overnight (8 hours), at weekends and/or during the day (3 hours).

   *'An eight-hour nightly shutdown could potentially save up to a third of the electrical energy used by a fan motor over the course of a season . . . A three-hour shutdown has the potential to save an eighth of the electrical energy used during a day.'*[17]

# Energy

- ★ Clean grilles and diffusers to remove the build-up of dust/dirt to maintain efficient operation.
- ★ Modify the relative humidity (RH) and temperature set points to provide wider control bands.
- ★ Use the collection to help with environmental control. Think about storage density. The more hygroscopic materials in a space, the more they reduce RH, thus reducing the need for mechanical control.
- ★ Dress for the weather. Reduce the need for heating by putting on a jumper. Reduce the need for cooling by wearing lightweight clothing. In other words, wear clothes that keep you warm when it's cold and cool when it's warm.
- ★ Install a communal blanket box for staff use on chilly days.
- ★ Shut the doors when it's cold. This keeps the room warm with less energy.
- ★ Make yourself a draft excluder. Nip down to the conservation studio and reuse those offcuts of polyester wadding, Tyvek and Plastazote to make your own, OR simply roll up some bubble wrap from packaging and tie with offcuts of tying tape!
- ★ Hang a curtain over a draughty door.
- ★ Close curtains or blinds at dusk in the winter to retain the heat in the room.
- ★ Close curtains or blinds on sunny days to keep rooms cooler by reducing solar gain.
- ★ Keep curtains and blinds closed in rooms that you're not using to keep them warm or cool depending on the weather.
- ★ Fit UV filtering film to windows to help keep rooms cooler.
- ★ Open a window for ventilation rather than switching on the desk fan.
- ★ Think about the layout of your workspace. Have you accidentally created an energy suck by placing a piece of equipment that generates heat next to equipment that needs to stay cool? Have you placed a piece of equipment which generates heat next to a

heating/cooling sensor? Are you reducing the efficiency of your heaters or fans because of where you have placed them?

- Refrigerators are affected by heat, so place them away from heat sources. They can consume 20% more energy if placed near a radiator.[18] Ideally, refrigerators should be placed 10 cm away from the wall.
- Keep the space around heaters clear to allow the heat to radiate.

★ Set the thermostat to 18ºC. The heat generated by people, IT equipment and lights will take it to 21ºC.
★ Suggest that the cleaners come in during the day. In this way, extra lighting and heating won't be needed in the evenings when the building is normally unoccupied.
★ Go into work at times when you wouldn't normally be there. You'll be able to spot energy being used that you weren't aware of and then be able to take steps to address this.

### Example:

♦ In one museum, the security lights in the exhibition areas were left on overnight and were brighter than the lighting used during the day. No one went into the exhibition areas when the museum was closed.

# 3 Water

You might be asking yourself how using water affects GHG emissions and the environment. Here are a few examples:

- 'Our use of water and energy are closely linked. Operational emissions from the water industry account for nearly 1% of the UK's total carbon emissions. This is because water treatment is energy and chemical intensive and transporting water around the country requires a great deal of pumping. Reducing your water use will therefore have an impact on your carbon footprint.'[19]
    - It is easy to think only in terms of clean water, but you should think about wastewater too. The treatment of wastewater also requires the use of fossil fuels. Wastewater treatment increases GHG emissions and reduces air quality.

  'By using less water you are saving energy because cleaning waste water (or 'grey water', as it's called) is an energy-intensive process.'[20]
- Heating the hot water that comes out of your taps is an energy-intensive process.
- Using water efficiently minimises the amount of additional water being taken out of rivers and aquifers, especially given that our demands are rising. (Demands are predicted to rise with climate

change causing hotter, drier summers and unpredictable rainfall at other times of the year.) Using water efficiently protects water resources and the wildlife that relies on them for its survival.

## Tips

★ Put up signs to encourage people to turn off the tap.

> 'Letting your faucet run for five minutes uses about as much energy as a 60-watt light bulb consumes in 14 hours.'[21]

★ Fix that dripping tap.

> 'A single dripping tap can waste up to 4 litres of water a day.'[22]

★ Put a brick in the water cistern of the toilet. You'll save a brick's volume in water every time you flush.

★ Contact your water supplier for free water saving devices. There are 100,000s of water saving devices available for free in the UK from the water suppliers. Check out 'Free water saving devices'.

> *https://www.moneysavingexpert.com/utilities/cut-water-bills/?utm_source=MSE_Newsletter&utm_medium=email&utm_term=02-Nov-21-50702448-14187&source=CRM-MSETIP-50702448&utm_campaign=nt-hiya&utm_content=9#gadgets*

★ Your water supplier may also offer water audits to see how efficient your water usage is. Some water suppliers offer a personalised water management package to get the best water efficiency plan for your organisation/business. Contact your water supplier to ask them what they offer.

★ Install a water meter. When you're paying your utility provider for exactly how much water you use, laid out in an itemised bill, there's an incentive to waste less!

- ★ Check your meters at night or when no water is being used to monitor for leakage.
- ★ Make sure you know where your supply pipes run and where the shut off valves are. That way, if you have a leak, you can turn everything off before you waste too much water AND there'll be less potential for water damage to your collection!
- ★ Make sure your pipes are protected against cold weather as leaks will increase with a burst pipe due to frost. AGAIN, this is of great benefit to your collection in reducing the potential for water damage.
- ★ Research water recycling schemes.
- ★ Determine where your waste water is going and whether or how you can recycle it in other areas of your organisation/business.

**Example:**

- ◆ Grey water can be used to wash vehicles/your bike/ muddy shoes and to water plants.

- ★ When running the tap from cold to get warm water, fill empty bottles or a watering can with the cold water. You can use this water in the kettle or to water your plants.
- ★ Only fill the kettle with the exact amount needed for the purpose.
- ★ Drink tap water.
- ★ Invest in water-efficient goods when you need to replace them. You can now get water-efficient showerheads, percussion or timed taps, toilets, washing machines and dishwashers.
- ★ Put water displacement devices in cisterns.
- ★ When washing your hands, turn the tap off whilst you are lathering up.
- ★ In the kitchen:

    o Wash up in a bowl. This will reduce the amount of water you use.

○ Fill a jug with tap water and place it in your fridge. This will mean you do not have to leave the cold tap running for the water to run cold before you fill your glass.

Studio roof garden watered with grey water

# 4 In your studio . . . the collection, your office and the kitchen

Let's take a second to reflect. Think about why. Why are you using that material, piece of equipment or solvent? Why are you working in that particular way? Are you doing it because you have always done it that way? Could you do it differently and more sustainably? Could you use a more sustainable material or solvent? Could you use less? Do you need to do it? Question the usual.

With any project, be it in your studio, the collection or your office, design for sustainability. In other words, design to refuse, reduce, reuse and recycle. An example of this is making adjustable book cradles which can be used in other exhibitions. Use alternatives to non-recyclable materials whenever possible, such as using mountboard with a starch adhesive, not a plastic-based adhesive. Use only easy-to-recycle materials; that could be book cradles made from board, not perspex.[23] Make your own rather than purchasing, such as cushions to support items. Designing for sustainability at the start of a project typically offers greater savings across a project's lifetime with regard to resources, labour and cost.

## Example:

◆ 'Tate Modern and Royal Academy of Arts trialled reusable exhibition walls in temporary exhibition spaces. This innovation in exhibition design eliminated the consumption, transport and disposal of over 600 sheets of medium density fibreboard per temporary exhibition.'[24]

It's time for the tips that you can use in your studio, the collection, your office and the kitchen. REMEMBER that the tips given already apply to everything you use, whether that's in the studio, the archive or your office. Use those tips and these tips too . . .

# Tips

### *In your studio and the collection*

★ Supports for items can be made using packaging chips from deliveries. Pop them into a bag to use. You could use surplus plastic bags or make bags from Tyvek offcuts.
   Bubble wrap from packaging also makes a good temporary support for books.
   The great thing about these methods is that you can make the support exactly the size and shape that you need it to be to fully support the item.
★ Reuse glass from display cases, and wooden boards from deliveries, to make pressing boards.
★ Make seal bags from Tyvek offcuts.
★ Bottles filled with sand, leather offcuts sewn into pouches and filled, covered bricks, milk bottles filled with sand (complete with useful handle!) can all be used as weights.

## In your studio... the collection, your office and the kitchen

- ★ Construct your own humidification chamber using the scratched perspex removed from framed items.
- ★ Reuse sheets of perspex as covers for humidity chambers.
- ★ Reuse sheets of perspex as a 'board' when lining items. (This means you can also move the item if you need to.)
- ★ Large cardboard boxes from deliveries make excellent cleaning cabinets.
- ★ Knit your own cleaning cloths to clean your studio (and your office and kitchen).
- ★ Make your own cleaning cloths to clean the studio (and your office and kitchen) from unwanted cotton t-shirts. Cut up, they make excellent, and very absorbent, cleaning cloths. You'll also stop difficult-to-recycle material going into the system. T-shirts with rubberised logos and images are difficult to recycle due to the polyurethane backing on the logo/image.
- ★ Coffee jars, pots, jam jars and contact lens pots can all be put to good use. There are many different ways you can reuse them. Here are a few examples:
  - o Contact lens pots are great for storing samples.
  - o Gü pots make great mixing pots.
    - → The lids from Pringles tubes and Bisto gravy canisters are a good fit for Gü pots, and they make them stackable, too.
  - o Jam jars are really useful for holding the water to clean your brushes in.
- ★ The lids from Dow Egbert jars make great containers for liquids if you remove the plastic bung. The tapered shape of the lid also lends itself to being anti-spill.
- ★ Reuse plastic takeaway trays. You can use them for:
  - o Storage

# Low Cost/No Cost Tips for Sustainability in Cultural Heritage

Reused pots and jars

- o Mini humidification chambers
- o Washing trays for small items
- o Holding any bits and pieces that you remove from an item. They can't roll off your bench, you have them all in one place and you can put the lid on the tray to keep them safe.
- o Reuse the small sachets of silica gel that come free with purchases such as shoes and handbags as a desiccant with small metal items.

★ Reuse the chopsticks that come with takeaway meals. They can be used as:

- o Stirrers
- o Spatulas. Whittle them down to make a bespoke bamboo spatula

## In your studio . . . the collection, your office and the kitchen

- o Quick builds around items, e.g. when making a temporary structure around an item when humidifying.

* Silvered paper lids from takeaway containers can be used as a reflector for small item photography.
* The small aluminium dishes that mince pies and cakes come in are ideal for mixing small quantities of paint, adhesive or filler, and for putting small objects or fragments in.
* Put your spare Really Useful boxes, or other plastic boxes, to good use. They make excellent humidification chambers.
* Put a blanket under the paper on your bench to pad the hard surface instead of Plastazote. Use old blankets from around your house or buy them from the charity shop.
* If you are examining/handling items with a lot of surface dirt and/or pests and you need to protect the surface you are working on, use lining paper for walls instead of blotters to cover the surface. You could even use spare patterned wallpaper turned pattern side down to cover surfaces.
* Take the weights out of old curtains and/or net curtains. You can use them in the studio and/or the archive to weigh down paper and parchment.
* Remove the ivory from the keys of an unwanted piano. This will give you 52 small, flexible bone folders.
* Gloves:
    - o Fill them with sand and use them as weights.
    - o Cut off cuffs and use these as rubber bands.
    - o Use latex gloves whenever possible because latex is biodegradable.
    - o Only wear gloves when you need to.
    - o Try to find replacements for materials, such as solvents, which require you to wear gloves.

- Use gloves as long as possible. Remember gloves can be washed.
- If gloves are still usable but are no longer suitable for use in the studio, use them for other jobs around your workplace, or take them home and use them there.

★ Scalpel blades and utility knife blades blunt quickly when cutting mountboard, but they are often sharp enough to be used for other jobs. Pop them into one of those jam jars and reuse, or give them to others to use.

★ Do you have papers that you can't use anymore? Perhaps you don't know what the papers are, or there might be papers which are out of date, such as Microchamber. There are many ways you can use these. Here are a few suggestions:

- lining work benches
- packing items temporarily, such as when returning them to clients or moving from one location to another
- as flip charts
- creating mind maps
- packing parcels in your workplace or at home
- donate to local artists or schools.

★ Pass on your offcuts by using the 'Put it on the Pavement with a Note' method.

★ You may be able to sell your offcuts. You might be surprised to learn that you can sell toilet roll tubes! 50 toilet rolls can make £5.00!! Check out this guide: "Flog your rubbish for cash".

*https://www.moneysavingexpert.com/family/flog-your-rubbish-for-cash/*

★ Turn off the fume cupboard and bench extraction when not in use.
★ Close the fume hood when in use.

In your studio ... the collection, your office and the kitchen

★ Do you like cake making or have a friend who is a whizz at cake decorating? Offcuts of polyester can be used instead of shop-bought acetate to apply decorations.

## In the office

★ Print less.

> 'The average UK office worker prints 6,000 sheets of paper a year, of which around 62% is wasted or unnecessary. Encourage staff to make use of digital tools and software that reduces the need for print, such as Adobe Sign or digital proofing tools, and produce more reports digitally. Also consider other initiatives such as setting the default on printers to printing black and white, and double-sided, or for even more of a challenge, try setting a maximum sheets-per-person printing target.'[25]

★ Consider the cost of printing. The cost of ink alone is roughly 20p per page for colour printers and 7.5p for B&W printers. The cost may stop you from printing. A sustainability win.

  o To estimate the cost per page, divide the price of an ink or toner cartridge by the number of pages the manufacturer states it should print. (Do exercise some caution with the estimate produced. Printer manufacturers base their figures on 5% of each printed page being covered in ink, whereas a full page of text is usually closer to 10%.)

★ Change the font when printing. Changing your font from Arial to Century Gothic will save 30% of ink used.
★ Switch off the photocopier.

> 'A photocopier left on stand-by mode overnight consumes enough energy to make 30 cups of tea.'[26]

- ★ Remove individual photocopiers and switch to a centralised, networked system.
- ★ Try to source photocopiers which use a low melting point toner. These can save up to 40% of the energy used by reducing the warm-up time.[27]
- ★ Use biodegradable vegetable photocopier inks.
- ★ Print on both sides of the paper.
  - o Put a box next to your copier/printer for the paper printed on one side only. It's readily to hand when you want to print on the other side.
- ★ Use certified products, such as FSC paper.
- ★ Use a paper with a lower gsm. Changing from 100 gsm to 80 gsm cuts consumption by 20%.[28]
- ★ Use paper with post-consumer recycled fibre.
- ★ Reuse paper. For example, old diaries can be used as notepads and notebooks, and the blank sides of delivery notes and invoices can be used as scrap paper for messages.
- ★ Reuse packaging materials from deliveries. If you reuse your packaging for other parcels, make others aware that you are doing this. Make a statement on the package such as 'Packed in 100% reused packaging' to inspire others and to demonstrate your sustainability actions to others.
- ★ Reuse A4 envelopes as folders for filing and for storing your papers and documents.
- ★ Cable tidies (which are usually made from plastic) can be replaced with leftover cotton tying tape, cut strips of old clothing or cut strips of used gloves.
- ★ Reduce your use of single-use items; e.g. replace disposable ballpoint pens with refillable ballpoint pens.

> 'Compared to a traditional disposable plastic pen, refillable pens reduce waste by about 50%.'[29]

## In your studio . . . the collection, your office and the kitchen

★ Encourage recycling by removing individual rubbish bins and replacing these with shared recycling bins.
★ Make a standing desk from old cardboard boxes.
★ Make a footrest from a cardboard packaging box. Cover it with some leftover wallpaper or unwanted paper from the studio to make it look nice. You can replace the cover when it gets worn.
★ Make your own business cards. You'll need a self-inking stamp with all the correct details and offcuts of paper and card from the studio.[30]
★ Create a reuse stop. This is an area where you can put anything that can be reused such as clean jam jars, packaging from parcels, tin cans, scrap paper, spare file dividers, files, etc. Have fun with it. For example, can you come up with a better name than reuse stop?
★ Put a box (reused of course) of spare plastic bags next to the office door. These bags can be reused by anyone nipping out at lunchtime.

Make your own business cards

★ Pass on unwanted office equipment and materials. You can use the 'Put it on the Pavement with a Note' method, offer it online or use a variety of other methods
★ Keep motivated and increase your sustainability efforts by having a competition with other departments, e.g. conservators vs curators, educators vs archivists or technicians vs HR. If you work on your own, team up with other lone workers and have a competition with them. Have fun!
★ Add some plants. Plants absorb $CO_2$, pollutants and toxins.
★ Check out 'How to Grow Fresh Air. 50 Houseplants that Purify Your Home or Office' by Dr B.C. Wolverton, 2008 and the NASA Clean Air Study.

*https://en.wikipedia.org/wiki/NASA_Clean_Air_Study*

★ Use pencil shavings in the garden as a pest deterrent (pencils are usually made of cedar wood). This will also add organic matter to the soil.

## In the kitchen

★ Replace paper towels with hand towels. Hand towels can be washed and reused.
★ Only boil the amount of water in the kettle that you need.

> *'If everyone boiled only the water they needed every time they used the kettle, we could save enough electricity in a year to power the UK's street lights for nearly seven months.'*[31]

★ Use plant-based cleaning products.
  o Non-plant-based cleaning products do not break down easily. They persist in the water system, accumulating, increasing in

concentration and combining with other chemicals. When they do break down, they release toxic compounds that are harmful to aquatic life and other wildlife.

★ Stop using disposables.

- o Fill the kitchen cupboard with reusable cups, mugs, glasses, plates and cutlery. Even better if you fill it with some beautiful sets from charity shops. You could have a mug amnesty where staff can bring in their spares from home.
- o Have a bowl of sugar rather than sachets and a bottle of milk/milk substitute rather than individual one-portion pots.
- o Ditch the disposable wipe. Knit your own or make your own from old clothes.

★ Use a refillable water bottle.

- o If you are out and about, there are many places where you can refill for free. The app (*https://www.refill.org.uk*) lists over 30,000 locations such as cafés, restaurants, shops, hotels and more which let you fill up your own bottle or flask, even if you're not a customer. You can use the app in Europe, the US, Australia, India and Singapore.

## *From the archive*

Think about what comes out of the stores for disposal. What do you do with these? Do you throw them away? Could you reuse them instead?

Think also about what the collections are packed in when they come into the studio, the archive and the museum. They are usually in all sorts of weird and wonderful containers which will be replaced.

What do you do with these containers? Do you throw them away? Could you reuse them instead?

Think also about items that collections contain which aren't relevant and won't be accessioned. What do you do with these? Do you throw them away? Could you reuse them instead?

Here are some ideas of how to reuse items:

- **Microfilm tins**. These make excellent containers for all sorts of things. You can reuse them in the studio, the office or at home.
- **Index card files**. Reuse them for business cards.
- **Deed boxes**. Reuse them to store packaging material, files, paper, envelopes and other office supplies.
- **Blind embossing stamps**. These make great paperweights and bookends in the office. They look really stylish, too.
- **Old storage boxes**. Boxes used to store collection material can become too scuffed and battered to continue to be used in the store. However, they are often still in good enough condition to be used to store office papers, handling collections and other materials.
- **Archive boxes**. Often suppliers of conservation and preservation materials will send your order in a surplus/seconds archive box. These surplus/seconds are difficult for the supplier to sell individually, but the boxes are perfectly good to use to store your collection in. You could also use them for the storage of your teaching/handling collection, to send out loans in, for returning items to clients or for moving items.
- **Crates and boxes**. You can reuse these in your office for storage or you can reuse them more imaginatively.
- **Photographic plate boxes**. Use these as part of your handling and/or teaching collection. You can also reuse these for storage for the bits and pieces in your office such as cables, chargers and pens.
- **Deaccessioned/non-accessioned items**. Add them to your handling and/or teaching collection.

In your studio . . . the collection, your office and the kitchen

What items can you add to this list? How can you reuse them? Could they be of use to others? Get creative.

Reusing items from the archive

43

# 5 Digital

If Information and Communications Technology was a country, it would be the third-highest consumer of electricity after the US and China. If the internet was a country, it would be the sixth-largest greenhouse gas polluter (equivalent to Australia, Denmark and the UK combined).[32]

Life in the digital age comes with a variety of environmental impacts:

- energy consumption from the manufacture of products and use of products, and by the communications network and the data centres
- mining of the minerals for the products
- e-waste dumps

To give you some context:

- 'Data centers [. . . are] capable of consuming as much power as a medium sized city.'[33]
- 'Global estimates of data center electricity demand in 2030 anticipate an increase of three to 10 times current levels, with high end estimates of projected data center electricity demand alone reaching 13% of global electricity consumption.'[34]

- In 2020 smartphone manufacture produced 130 million tonnes of $CO_2$, which is equivalent to the annual emissions of the Philippines.[35]
- Mining is water-intensive, and causes deforestation and land degradation. For example, coltan, a key ingredient of many electronics, is mined in the Democratic Republic of Congo in gorilla habitat, disrupting that habitat and leading to the poaching of gorillas.[36]
- Our devices contain conflict minerals. These are minerals which are mined in areas of armed conflict and human rights abuses.[37]

Some of the major companies have taken steps to act sustainably, and they continue to do so. For example, 'Apple and Google continue to lead the sector in matching their growth with an equivalent or larger supply of renewable energy, and both companies continue to use their influence to push governments as well as their utility and IT sector vendors to increase access to renewable energy for their operations.'[38] In 2017, Google used 100% renewable energy and was carbon neutral for its data centres and offices. In 2018, Apple used 100% renewable energy and was carbon neutral for its data centres, offices and retail shops.[39] 'Microsoft recently pledged that by 2050 it will have removed more carbon from the atmosphere (and presumably continue to do so) than it will have caused since its founding in 1975.'[40]

As ever, it is important to check the data produced by these companies to ensure that they are meeting their pledges and to ascertain what they actually mean by renewable energy and carbon neutral.

## Tips

★ Move data to the cloud.

- ○ Moving data to the cloud delivers 72% to 93% carbon savings in comparison to traditional computing.[41]
- ○ A shift to cloud-based could mean a 38% reduction in energy usage.[42]

★ Switch to cloud services and web hosting that are powered by renewable sources and are transparent and accountable on their energy sources, GHG emissions and targets. Check out the 'Green Hosting Directory' to find one.

*https://thegreenwebfoundation.org*

★ Limit reply all.
★ Remove unnecessary text and/or content from emails, including the chain of messages, photographs, logo, images in the footer and 'Think Before You Print'.
★ Reduce the number of messages that you send.

- ○ One email releases 4 grams of $CO_2$ into the atmosphere. An email with a large attachment could have a footprint of up to 50 grams.[43]
- ○ A year of incoming mail for a typical business creates around 135 kg of $CO_2$.[44]

★ Delete old messages in your email.
★ Unsubscribe from newsletters that you no longer read and groups that you no longer want to be part of.
★ Delete all apps, email subscriptions and online services you no longer use.

- Delete items from your bin.
- Turn off your video during online meetings.
- Dim your monitor.
  - 'Reducing your PC monitor brightness from 100% to 70% can save up to 20% of the energy the monitor uses.'[45]

- Avoid screensavers.
  - Screensavers do not save energy.

  *'Most screensavers use the same amount of energy as when the screen is in normal use.'*[46]

- Shut down your computer if you are away from it for more than two hours.
  - 'The average desktop computer can cost around £45 per year to run if it is left on 24/7. This can be reduced to £12 if it is turned off when not in use, at night, and on weekends/vacations.'[47]

- Set your computer to go into sleep mode after a set period of inactivity.
- Set your mobile to go onto auto lock after a set amount of time.
- Unplug your devices when you are not using them. They continue to draw on the power when they are plugged in but powered down.
- Remove your devices from the power when they are charged. They continue to draw on the power when fully charged.
- Unplug chargers when you have finished using them.
- Use a tablet or a smartphone instead of a laptop or desktop because they use less power.
- Replace your desktops with laptops (when upgrading). They

use around 20% less energy than a desktop and there won't be a need to buy additional equipment for use when you are working offsite.
★ Choose the most energy-efficient digital devices.
★ Use your mobile on wi-fi rather than 4G.

   o '4G consumes 4x more energy than wi-fi.'[48]

★ Go straight to a website rather than using a search engine. Add the websites that you use frequently to your bookmarks or favourites.

   o A search emits 0.2 grams of $CO_2$. Based on the average of 3.5B searches per day, that's 700 tonnes of $CO_2$ emissions daily![49]

★ Switch search engines.

   o Ecosia is a search engine that plants trees. 45 searches = 1 tree.

   *https://www.ecosia.org*

★ Browse wisely.

   o Loading the average website uses as much energy as that required for boiling the water for a cup of tea.

★ Clear out your browser history.
★ Browse incognito. Tightening your privacy options will decrease tracking, reducing energy use and thus reducing GHG emissions.
★ Reduce the number of tabs you have open.
★ Check your website's carbon footprint. You could try *https://www.websitecarbon.com*
★ If you need to purchase a new device, buy one that has the least impact.

- Fairphone uses Fairtrade certified gold. They are also acting to source conflict-free tin, tungsten and tantalum.
- Fairphone phones are built with a modular design so that the parts can be replaced. They also use some recycled plastics.

  https://www.fairphone.com/en/

- Apple, Google, HP and Microsoft are all working to source conflict-free minerals.
- Apple has announced that self-service repair is available for iPhone 12 and iPhone 13.

★ Opt for a refurbished device, use it for as long as possible, repair and pass it on to someone else when it has reached the end of its usable life with you or recycle.

- Check out:

  → **Computeraid** for how to pass on devices that you no longer need for reuse and/or recycling.

  https://www.computeraid.org/about-us

  → **Reconome** for recycling smartphones.

  https://recycle.recono.me

  → **Apple** for the recycling of Apple products.

  www.apple.com/uk/recycling/nationalservice

  → **Microsoft** for their recycling programme for Microsoft-branded consumer products and/or its packaging.

  https://www.microsoft.com/en-us/legal/compliance/recycling

★ Think about all the ancillaries that you use as part of your digital life. This includes headphones, earbuds, mobile phone cases, screen protectors, laptop bags, cables, cables, cables, chargers, plugs, memory sticks . . . The list is almost endless.

Do you need more? Can you use what you already have? Could you source pre-loved items? Can you make your own? Get crafty with your Tyvek offcuts and bubble wrap to make a laptop bag. What else could you make? Get creative.

Handmade laptop case made from offcuts of felt and ribbons from packaging

# 6  Travel and Transport

Commuting contributes to 5% of total UK GHG emissions. A journey of 5 to 50 miles is the worst emitter.[50] The travel and transport that takes place as part of your work is not only commuting; there are many other instances. These include:

- Couriering of items
- Attendance of meetings
- Attendance of conferences
- Working at another site
- Visiting clients
- Visiting to view items in situ
- Collecting materials and equipment
- How your visitors travel to you
- How your colleagues, specialists, service engineers and other work visitors travel to you

What other travel and transport do you do that you can add to this list? What measures can you take to reduce the amount that you travel, the impact of your travel and the impact of those that travel to you?

Low Cost/No Cost Tips for Sustainability in Cultural Heritage

## Tips

★ Walk, cycle or use public transport to get to work.
★ Walk, cycle or use public transport when travelling for work. It may take you longer but explain this. Explain to those you are meeting that you are not driving to the meeting for environmental reasons.

Use the train

★ Organise meetings and/or events in places that are accessible by public transport.

- Be flexible over the start and end times of meetings/events. This will allow more people to use public transport because:
    → they'll be able to avoid expensive peak travel tickets
    → those who have a more restricted public transport network will be able to get to and from meetings/events using it.
- If you are organising an event where using the car is necessary (even if it is the last bit from the train station to the venue), help delegates to arrange this with one another before the meeting and/or organise a minibus.

★ Hold your meetings online or use the phone whenever possible.
★ Hold your events online whenever possible.
★ Work from home when possible.
★ Car share if the car is the only option.
★ If you need to use a car:

- Avoid speeding, rapid acceleration, sudden braking, revving the engine and staying in a low gear. These all increase fuel consumption.
- Open a window to stay cool if you are driving at a slow speed. Over 50 mph, use the air-conditioning.
- Make sure the tyres are correctly inflated.
- Remove the roof rack.
- Give your car a good clear out. Anything that adds weight to your car increases fuel consumption.
    Check out 'Green Driving Tips' for more ideas on how to reduce the impact of driving. There's also a poster of tips to download.

    *https://www.eta.co.uk/driving-tips/*

- ★ If you use a hire car, select an electric car.
- ★ Use taxi firms with electric cars.
- ★ Use bicycle couriers.
- ★ Avoid flying. If you must fly:
  - o Fly economy to maximise efficiency.
  - o Fly direct to minimise excessive emissions created during takeoff and landing.
  - o Fly during the daytime to cut down on creating heat-trapping contrail and cirrus clouds at night.

- ★ Develop a travel policy, e.g. over 10 hours = flight, anything less = train.
  - o If you do develop a travel policy, make sure that everyone you work with is aware of it. Add a prompt to remind yourself and your colleagues when you are booking tickets to search for the method that has the least impact on the climate.

- ★ Share knowledge with one another about how to get to work without needing to drive. Sharing knowledge will also encourage and inspire those who may be feeling less confident to give alternative modes of transport a go. You could share details of the best cycle routes, how to avoid that tricky roundabout when cycling, and the location of EV charging points.
  - o There are numerous ways to share knowledge. How about over lunch, organising a weekly transport chat, in the staff meeting and at networking and business events? Have fun doing this.

- ★ Tell others about your transport and travel choices if you have found an alternative to driving.

## Travel and Transport

★ Let your visitors know how they can get to you without using their car, whether that's by walking, cycling and/or public transport.
   o Add these details to your website and/or replies to emails.
   o You can also add information about accessible transport options.

★ Survey your colleagues and your visitors about how they travel to you.
★ Seek feedback from your colleagues and your visitors. They might want to use public transport but don't because the bus doesn't link up sensibly with the train or because the buses stop running too early. They might respond that they would have cycled if only they'd known that a cycle path existed.
★ Put alternative travel choices on the agenda for the next team meeting to get the discussion started for both your colleagues and your visitors.
★ Check your existing facilities; e.g. if you have a cycle shed, is it used?
★ Check whether your employer is part of the Cycle to Work scheme. If they are, you can get a discount on a bike and accessories.

   *https://www.cycle2work.info*

★ Stay motivated and motivate others by taking part in national campaigns such as National Walking Week.
★ Keep your motivation high and, as always, have fun by holding competitions, such as how long will it take for you and your colleagues to walk the length of Hadrian's Wall, the Great Wall of China or to the moon!

# 7 Money

When you think about the steps you can take to reduce your impact on the climate and the environment, your money is probably one of the last areas you think about. It really is one of the most important. 'Greening your money' features in all the 'Top 10' lists of actions that you can take to reduce your GHG emissions.

> *'Research on behalf of Make My Money Matter found redirecting your pension wealth could have 21 times the impact on your carbon emissions than going vegetarian or giving up flying.'*[51]

The finance sector invests your money to make money. Your money could be invested in oil, coal, gas, airlines, deforestation, tobacco and weapons. The finance sector also wields great power. It can exert its influence to 'enable and accelerate the transition to a low-carbon and climate-resilient future . . . [including] stopping the financing and investing in fossil energy extraction, virgin fossil materials and deforestation, increasing investments in new green technologies and using the power as owners and lenders to influence company behaviours and disclosure practises,'[52] or it can support the status quo, condemning us all.

> 'The Bank of England recently noted that the global financial system supports carbon-producing projects that, if left unchecked, will cause a global temperature rise of more than 4°C.'[53]

The focus in finance is on divestment. That is, moving investment from climate-damaging sectors to low-carbon sectors. It may sound counter-intuitive but there is an argument to be made for investing in carbon-heavy sectors such as industrials, materials and infrastructure to allow our money to be used to find solutions that enable these sectors to become net-zero. Check out this great TED talk for more information: The Crucial Intersection of Climate and Capital.[54]

*https://www.ted.com/talks/nili_gilbert_the_crucial_intersection_of_climate_and_capital?language=en*

These are the areas you should think about regarding using your money to reduce your impact on the climate and the environment:

- **Banking**
  You might be thinking that there's nothing you can do to change who your employer banks with? Fair enough, but what about who you bank with? You can change that. If you run your own business, who do you bank with for both your business and your personal account? How do they rank for sustainability?
  Don't forget about your credit card and loans!

- **Insurance**
  Insurance 'is a vital actor on environmental issues . . . First, it is one of the largest investors in the financial markets, with long-term obligations through health and life insurance and pensions. Second, the industry acts as an informal regulator. Insurers can demand changes in corporate, personal and even government behaviour in return for lower premiums and novel approaches to

underwriting risks. They can demand better climate change and adaptation measures.'[55]

> '*The path insurers choose to take will be central to our collective chances of meeting the environmental challenges. . . . The sooner everyone realises that, and finds ways to encourage insurers to do the right thing, the better.*'[56]

- **Pensions**
  'One area with enormous, untapped potential to turn the tide is . . . pensions. £2.6 trillion is invested in pensions in the UK alone. That's our money. It does not belong to hedge fund managers, or government, or billionaire CEOs worried about the size of their rockets. It belongs to every single citizen saving up for the future. To us.'[57]

  Globally, pensions account for half the money in the world. Collectively we have the power.

It is easy to green your money. There are guides and resources to help you through the process. Here are a few you might like to check out:

- 'Fossil Free Funds.'

  *https://fossilfreefunds.org*

- 'Green Investing: How your savings can fight climate change.'

  *https://www.bbc.co.uk/news/business-58544966*

- 'Most Ethical Banks in the UK 2021 (Plus the ones to avoid).'

  *https://www.tinyecohomelife.com/most-ethical-banks-uk*

- '19 Green MoneySaving tips.'

    *https://www.moneysavingexpert.com/news/2021/11/martins-19-green-saving-tips/?utm_source=MSE_Newsletter&utm_medium=email&utm_term=09-Nov-21-50703373-13160&source=CRM-MSETIP-50703373&utm_campaign=nt-oneliners-one&utm_content=11*

- 'Pension Power: What in the world is our money building?'

    *https://shareaction.org/savers-resource-hub/pension-power-what-world-is-our-money-building*

- 'The Good Guide to Pensions.'

    *https://good-with-money.com/wp-content/uploads/2019/08/The-Good-Guide-to-Pensions-2019-FINAL1.pdf*

It is important to be aware that this is a rapidly moving sector. Do your research, seek financial advice, ask friends and colleagues for their recommendations and keep an eye on your providers.

### Example:

- ◆ A UK bank which for many years has been regarded as an 'ethical' bank was recently bought by a US bank which invests in fossil fuels, airlines and weapons. It no longer features in any of the lists detailing recommendations for 'ethical' banks.

## Tips

★ If you move your money, tell your provider why. The more we bring sustainability to their attention, the more likely they'll be to change.
★ Ask your providers what funds your money is invested in. Even if you can't move it, it brings sustainability to their attention, meaning that they are more likely to change.
★ If you have a pension, ask which funds your pension is invested in.
  - If you discover that your pension is invested in funds that perpetuate the climate crisis, ask how you can change those funds and do it.
★ Contact your bank, insurer and pension provider and request that they align their investments with the Paris Agreement. Pressure them to stop investing in projects which damage the climate and the environment.

*'Consumer decisions influence markets.'*[58]

# 8 Inspiring others/ Influencing stakeholders/ Changing behaviour

Have you taken sustainability actions? Did you share your actions and successes with your colleagues and peers? In the cultural heritage sector, we are not good at celebrating our achievements. When did you see a fellow professional shouting their brilliant sustainability actions from the rooftops? Yet the cultural heritage sector is creative and full of people finding innovative solutions to the climate and the environment crises. By sharing your actions, no matter how small, you inspire and encourage others. The act of doing something and taking action causes others to take action. It creates behavioural contagion. What you do and say changes others. It spreads the word and sparks and sustains dialogue.

### Ask, Inspire, Encourage, Share

All conversations are good, even if the reaction to them is negative. Your actions may be questioned, your statistics, thoughts or suggested sustainability steps may not be well received, but don't worry; what's most important is getting the conversation started. The first step is to get your colleagues and peers thinking about the issues and discussing them.

### Talk, Discuss, Debate, Share

Speaking about your successes, sharing your actions with others, speaking up, talking about what we can do, asking why action hasn't been taken and holding others accountable are all ways that you can inspire others, influence stakeholders and change behaviour.

### Act

'For the commitment [to net zero by 2050] to be realised, we need the behaviours of the whole country to change. Individuals, companies and communities need to see the role they can play and commit to that role.'[59]

## Tips

- ★ Read your organisation's vision and mission statements, and suggest statements to be included that reflect your organisation's commitment to sustainability.
- ★ Ensure that your sustainability statement/policy is easily accessible to everybody, including all your colleagues and those outside your organisation.
- ★ Put a short statement of your sustainability actions on your website and share it on your socials.

- ★ Explain why sustainability matters to you and your work.
- ★ Advocate for change.
- ★ Involve everyone, including housekeeping, Front of House, Security, Line Managers, the Director, visitors, clients and suppliers.
- ★ Assign roles and responsibilities. Give your colleagues designated roles and responsibilities for sustainability efforts and responsibility for monitoring progress. This will ensure that everyone feels involved. It will also prevent your colleagues from feeling that sustainability is the responsibility only of those with sustainability in their job title. EVERY JOB IS A CLIMATE JOB.
- ★ Find your allies. You can share your ideas and support and motivate one another.
- ★ Take every opportunity to put out positive sustainability messages. This will keep the dialogue around sustainability going.
- ★ The more we speak about sustainability, the more change we will create. It's important that others see us practising sustainability. In this way, they can copy us and they know it's OK.
- ★ Share your knowledge and experiences:
    - ○ contribute to conferences and panels
    - ○ write an article and/or blog
    - ○ post on social media

Tell the story of your sustainability journey. You could cover where you are now, where you are going and what you have left to do. Be honest. Don't be afraid to say what hasn't worked. Others will have made mistakes. Explaining what hasn't worked will help others to learn. You could also mention areas that you are finding difficult. Others may have the answer.
- ★ Talk about climate change and the environment. If you work in an organisation, ask if there is a sustainable energy policy, a sustainability strategy, a preferred purchases list, or a green materials list for exhibitions and what sustainability planning is taking place.

- ★ Talk to everyone, including those outside your workplace, other sector professionals and the museum's visitors. This will bring new ideas.

    **Example:**
    - ◆ A sustainability webinar sparked ideas for collaborations to share materials, to redistribute unwanted materials and generated lots of tips for practical actions.

- ★ Talk to those who can effect change, such as facilities, your manager, your suppliers, your insurance provider and your energy supplier.
- ★ Highlight the fact that profound change at a rapid pace is not only possible but has already occurred, i.e. Covid-19.
- ★ Be solutions focused.
- ★ Use positive messages.
- ★ Keep it simple.
- ★ Explain that sustainability actions will save money; e.g. we reduced our energy by X, which is enough to pay an apprentice for Y.

    **Example:**
    - ◆ 'If all students at Cambridge only filled their kettles to the amount needed it could save the University £80,000 on electricity bills.'[60]

- ★ Convert facts and figures into images.

    **Example:**
    - ◆ 'If all students at Cambridge only filled their kettles to the amount needed we could avoid the equivalent in greenhouse gas emissions of 16 London–Paris flights each year.'[61]

### Inspiring others/Influencing stakeholders/Changing behaviour

★ Celebrate your successes. Let others know what you have done. Share your successes both in your organisation and in the sector.
★ Make sure that your sustainability successes are shared with your visitors and clients.
★ Ask. Question your organisation, your suppliers, your transport providers, etc. about their commitments to sustainability and their actions. Only by asking and pushing for change, speaking up and making ourselves heard will change happen.

# 9 Recycling

Recycling used to be the go-to for sustainability, but now it is last on the list. Before putting any material or equipment into the recycling, think about how it can be reused.

The reason that recycling is last on the list is that recycling produces GHG emissions. It takes energy to make a material into something else (including collecting it from you and taking it to the recycling depot), and (usually) not all of the material can be recovered, meaning that some virgin materials will need to be added.

When you have got to the point that your materials and equipment can no longer be repaired, reused or handed on, then DO recycle. Recycling saves energy, reduces the demand for raw materials, reduces the burden on landfill and cuts GHG emissions.

Here are a few examples of the benefits of recycling:

- 'By recycling an aluminium can, 95% of the energy needed to make one from raw materials is saved. For paper, this is between 25 and 50%.'[62]
- 'Recycling ink/toner cartridges saves nearly 9600 kg of aluminium, 40 tons of plastic, and one million litres of oil for every 100,000 cartridges recycled.'[63]
- 'Compared to virgin paper, each ton (1000kg) of recycled

paper can save 17 trees, 380 gallons of oil, three cubic yards of landfill space, 4000 kilowatts of energy, and 7000 gallons of water.'[64]

## Tips

★ Make it easy for you and your colleagues to recycle.
★ Remove individual waste bins and install communal recycling bins.
★ Flatten cardboard boxes, drink cans and plastic bottles before recycling. This will save space in the collection vehicle and cut down on the number of trips to the plant and thus will lower GHG emissions of transporting recycling.
★ Sort. A few rogue items in the recycling will condemn the whole load to landfill or incineration because the waste plants don't have the time or the money to sort the load.

There are materials which are difficult to recycle, such as plastics, electrical items and gloves. These troublesome materials are especially difficult to recycle if you work on your own, and even more so if you can't get to your local recycling centre.

Find out what you can recycle locally and what you can do with items that you are unsure about at Recycle Now.

*https://www.recyclenow.com*

## Batteries

★ Recycle at supermarkets and all high street stores

## Lightbulbs

★ B&Q and Tesco

　○ B&Q: energy saving, incandescent and fluorescent
　○ Tesco: energy saving

## Small Electrical Items

★ B&Q

## Gloves

These are difficult to recycle if you work on your own. The recycling schemes are not free, costing £139 for a small box.

For those of you who generate enough gloves to make paying for a recycling box viable:

→ Terracycle takes gloves made from nitrile, latex, vinyl and plastic. They take all brands of gloves.

→ Kimberley Clarke (Rightcycle program) takes only their brand. They also take their own brand safety glasses and other PPE.

★ If you are unable to recycle your gloves because they are contaminated, cut out the contaminated areas and put the uncontaminated pieces in the glove recycling box.

## Masks

★ Single-use, disposable face masks can be recycled at Wilko. Find out more about the scheme at

*https://www.wilko.com/face-mask-recycling.*

## Plastics

★ Soft plastics such as packaging from deliveries, plastic bags that are no longer usable and bubble wrap can be recycled at supermarkets, including Sainsbury's and the Co-Operative. Tesco provides recycling for crisp packets and plastic film.

　○ Sealed Air offers a take back programme. Find out more at

　　*https://www.sealedair.com*

★ Used bottles made from PET can be filled with non-recyclable plastic for use as a building material. Find out more at

*https://www.ecobricks.org.*

★ Perspex. Most of the companies which manufacture Perspex offer a take back scheme.
★ Plastazote. The supplier, Kewell Converters, will take offcuts for reuse.
★ Tubes, bottles, sprays, caps, pumps and more can be recycled at Boots and Superdrug.

　Boots: *https://www.boots.com/shopping/boots-recycling-scheme*

　Superdrug: *https://www.superdrug.com/blog/new-and-trending/recycle-beauty-empties/*

## Work shoes and clothes

★ Clarks, in collaboration with Unicef, take any shoes, of any size and any brand. They use the funds raised to build schools and buy bicycles to help children get to school.
★ Take them to your local charity shop. Shoes and clothes which can't be sold in the shop are put in the 'rag bag'. The charity is paid for the 'rag bag' and the clothes are reused for padding for car seats and chairs.

## Office equipment

★ Inkjet cartridges

   o **Support Your School**: *www.supportyourschool.org.uk*
   o **Tesco**

★ Mobile phones

   o **Reconome**: *https://recycle.recono.me*

★ Computers

   o **Computeraid**: *https://www.computeraid.org/about-us*
   o **Apple**: *www.apple.com/uk/recycling/nationalservice*
   o **Microsoft**: *https://www.microsoft.com/en-us/legal/compliance/recycling*

## Aluminium cans and foil

You can recycle your empty aluminium drink cans and aluminium foil and make money! One kilo of cans equals 40 to 50 pence. (A kilo is usually 65 to 75 cans.)

- A recycled aluminium can saves enough energy to run a television for three hours.
- If all the aluminium drinks cans sold in the UK were recycled, there would be 14 million fewer dustbins.

**Think Cans**: *https://thinkcans.net/cash-cans/getting-started*

**Every Can Counts**: *https://everycancounts.co.uk/about-us/*

**AluCan Recycling**: *https://www.alucan.org.uk*

# 10 Think

'The definition of insanity is doing the same thing over and over again and expecting different results.'
                                  **Wrongly attributed to Albert Einstein**

★ Think about why. Why are you using that material, piece of equipment, solvent, water-intensive treatment, supplier or bank, for example? Why are you working in that particular way? Are you doing it because you always have? Is it because it's the best method? Is it the most efficient method? Is it the most sustainable method? Could you do it differently? Could you use something different which is more sustainable? Could you use less? Question the usual.

'Of all the forces in the universe, the hardest to overcome is the force of habit.'
                                                **Solomon Einstein[65]**

★ Think about who your professional membership is with. Join only those professional bodies who are committed to sustainability and who have a sustainability policy.

    o Some professional bodies now offer you the option of opting out of hard copy newsletters and journals in favour of online access. Check whether your professional body offers this. Opt out for sustainability if this suits you.

★ Think about your collections policy. Incorporate sustainability into the guidance on the transfer or donation of records. Do not collect indiscriminately. Deaccession.
★ Learn. Sign up for newsletters, training and webinars on sustainability. Learn as much as you can and pass it on.
★ Think about food. It is interesting that you hear a lot about reducing emissions from electricity production but you hear little about food and agriculture, yet they are almost similar in the amount of GHGs that they produce. Food accounts for 70% of global biodiversity loss and around a third of global GHG emissions. What can you do to reduce the climate and environmental impacts of food?

   Here are some suggestions:

   o Cater meetings and/or events with at least 50% of the food served as vegan.
   o Cater meetings and/or events vegetarian as default.
   o Serve less meat but of a better quality (i.e. free-range, organic, high-welfare).
   o Cater using locally sourced food and drink.
   o Cater organic.
   o If serving biscuits and snacks, make sure that they contain only RSPO-certified sustainable palm oil. Or better still, no palm oil at all.
   o Serve food that has achieved certification such as Fair Trade and Soil Association.

★ Measure. Calculate your carbon footprint to set a baseline from which you can see what you need to change. It will also allow you to see the positive effect of all the changes that you make. Once you know the size of your footprint, you can reduce it. Look at your average annual footprint, then set targets to reduce it. You could start small with a goal of reducing travel emissions by 5% over the next 3 years. You can also set targets that aren't emissions-based, such as reducing energy or water use by 2% a year. Set ambitious but achievable targets and report against these publicly. This shows your dedication to the environment, your responsibility for your impacts, and that you're willing to be held accountable.

# Let's wrap up . . .

'Never interrupt someone doing what you said couldn't be done.'
**Amelia Earhart**

So there you are. You now have lots of sustainability actions that you can take for low cost or no cost. You can put these into action today. Here's a challenge for you. What one tip will you put into action as soon as you put this book down?

Make sure that you celebrate your success when you take action. Put it on your socials and tell your colleagues. Remember that your actions inspire others to take action.

'No matter what our place in society, important problems don't get fixed until enough ordinary people mobilize to take action.'[66]

'That person who helps others simply because it should or must be done, and because it is the right thing to do, is indeed without doubt, a real superhero.'
**Stan Lee**

I'd love to hear your feedback and any tips you'd like to share on Twitter @conserve_lfcp and Instagram @thecaringconservator

And please come and visit me at lfcp.co.uk. You can keep up to date with the latest sustainability actions.

## Together we will make a difference.

Our beautiful planet

'You have left the world much better than you found it, nobody could do better than that.'
DEATH to Granny Weatherwax[67]

# Notes

## Let's get started

1. Christine Figueres. Conversation. RSA Journal. Issue 1. 2020. p.19
2. Sarah S. Brophy and Elizabeth Wylie. The Green Museum. A Primer on Environmental Practice, Second Edition. 2013. p.17
3. Going Green. Equity Newsletter. 24th June 2021
4. Megan de Silva and Jane Henderson. Sustainability in Conservation Practice. Journal of the Institute of Conservation. Volume 34. Number 1. 2011. p.6
5. Dr Jane Goodall. TED Global. 2007. Accessed August 2021
6. Brophy and Wylie. The Green Museum. p.17

## 1. Equipment and Materials

7. Shady Ships. Retail Giants Pollute Communities and Climate with Fossil-Fueled Ocean Shipping. 2021. p.22 https://www.pacificenvironment.org/wp-content/uploads/2021/07/SIZ_Shady-Ships-Report.pdf. Accessed September 2021
8. Shady Ships. Retail Giants Pollute Communities and Climate with Fossil-Fueled Ocean Shipping, loc. cit., p.22
9. Project Drawdown. Climate Solutions 101, 2021. https://drawdown.org/climate-solutions-101. Accessed July 2021
10. The Value of Re-using Household Waste Electrical and Electronic Equipment. 2011 www.wrap.org.uk/sites/files/wrap/WRAP%20WEEE%20HWRC%20summary%20report.pdf. Accessed October 2021

11. Lauren Wiseman. Let's make our workplace sustainable. World Wide Fund for Nature https://www.wwf.org.uk/updates/top-20-tips-workplaces-sustainable. Accessed October 2021
12. Lauren Wiseman. Let's make our workplace sustainable, loc. cit.
13. https://www.sustainable-markets.org/TerraCarta_Charter_Jan11th2021.pdf. Accessed January 2021

## 2. Energy

14. https://www.environment.admin.cam.ac.uk/facts-figures#lighting. Accessed November 2021
15. https://energysavingtrust.org.uk. Accessed November 2021
16. https://energysavingtrust.org.uk.
17. Sarah S. Brophy and Elizabeth Wylie. The Green Museum. A Primer on Environmental Practice, Second Edition. 2013. p.10
18. Energy. A Step-by-Step Guide for Sustainable Action. Vol. 1. Ki Culture. January 2021. p.49

## 3. Water

19. Waterwise. https://www.waterwise.org.uk/save-water/. Accessed November 2021
20. Water Saving Tips. Eden Project. https://www.edenproject.com/learn/eden-at-home/water-saving-tips. Accessed November 2021
21. Green Tips. World Wide Fund for Nature. https://www.worldwildlife.org/pages/green-tips. Accessed November 2021
22. Anna Shepard. How Green Are My Wellies? Small steps and giant leaps to green living with style. 2008. p.233

## 4. In your studio . . . the collection, your office and the kitchen

23. Perspex is a trade name for Poly Methyl Methacrylate [PMMA]. It's also referred to as acrylic, lucite or plexiglas.
24. Megan de Silva and Jane Henderson. Sustainability in Conservation Practice. Journal of the Institute of Conservation. Volume 34. Number 1. 2011. p.7
25. Lauren Wiseman. Let's make our workplace sustainable. World Wide Fund for

Nature. https://www.wwf.org.uk/updates/top-20-tips-workplaces-sustainable. Accessed November 2021
26. The Carbon Trust. https://www.carbontrust.com. Accessed November 2021
27. https://www.environment.admin.cam.ac.uk/facts-figures#lighting
28. Paper and the Environment. Julie's Bicycle. 2015. p.5. https://juliesbicycle.com/resource-paper-environment-2015/. Accessed November 2021
29. https://www.treehugger.com. Accessed October 2021
30. From SiConserve
31. Energy Saving Trust. https://energysavingtrust.org.uk

## 5. Digital

32. Environmental Sustainability in the Digital Age of Culture. Opportunities, Impacts and Emerging Practices. Julie's Bicycle. 2020. https://juliesbicycle.com/category/resource_hub/. Accessed December 2020
33. Clicking Green. Who is Winning the Race to Build a Green Internet? Greenpeace. 2017. p.17 http://www.clickclean.org. Accessed December 2020
34. Clicking Green, Greenpeace. 2017, p.17
35. Environmental Sustainability in the Digital Age of Culture. Julie's Bicycle. 2020. p.12
36. Sarah S. Brophy and Elizabeth Wylie. The Green Museum. A Primer on Environmental Practice, Second Edition. 2013. p.21
37. Environmental Sustainability in the Digital Age of Culture, Julie's Bicycle. 2020. p.12
38. Clicking Green. Greenpeace. 2017. p.7
39. A Guide to Global Internet Energy Usage. Energy Helpline. https://www.energyhelpline.com/help/a-guide-to-global-internet-energy-usage. Accessed November 2021
40. Tom Rippon. On Purpose. RSA Journal. Issue 1. 2020. p.21
41. Environmental Sustainability in the Digital Age of Culture. Julie's Bicycle. 2020
42. Environmental Sustainability in the Digital Age of Culture, loc. cit.
43. A Guide to Global Internet Energy Usage. Energy Helpline.
44. A Guide to Global Internet Energy Usage. Energy Helpline.
45. https://www.environment.admin.cam.ac.uk/facts-figures#lighting
46. https://www.environment.admin.cam.ac.uk/resources/mythbusters-facts-top-tips/screens

47. Greening the Office. Julie's Bicycle. 2015. p.6 https://juliesbicycle.com/category/resource_hub/. Accessed June 2021
48. Environmental Sustainability in the Digital Age of Culture. Opportunities, Impacts and Emerging Practices. Julie's Bicycle. 2020. p.18
49. A Guide to Global Internet Energy Usage. Energy Helpline.

## 6. Travel and Transport

50. Mobility Ways – Zero Carbon Commuting. James Shepherd. Webinar. 11th March 2021

## 7. Money

51. Lucy Hooker. Green Investing: How your savings can fight climate change. https://www.bbc.co.uk/news/business-58544966. Accessed November 2021
52. The 1.5°C Business Playbook. 2021. pp.6-7. https://exponentialroadmap.org/1-5c-business-playbook/. Accessed June 2021
53. Climate Solutions at Work. An Employee Guide to Drawdown Aligned Business. Project Drawdown. September 2021. p.29
54. Nili Gilbert. The Crucial Intersection of Climate and Capital. TED. https://www.ted.com/talks/nili_gilbert_the_crucial_intersection_of_climate_and_capital?language=en. Accessed December 2021
55. Ian Kearns and Peter Kingsley. Risky Business. RSA Journal. Issue 1. p.34
56. Ian Kearns and Peter Kingsley, Risky Business, RSA Journal. Issue 1. p.35
57. Will Attenborough. The Equity Pension is Changing for the Greener. https://www.equity.org.uk/news/2021/october/the-equity-pension-is-changing-for-the-greener/?link_id=3&can_id=af29b3f6abeb95c5096e78ccf68519f7&source=email-discrimination-at-work-your-right-to-equal-treatment&email_referrer=email_1325063&email_subject=equitys-pension-scheme-is-changing-for-the-greener-_ Accessed November 2021
58. Anna Shepard. How Green Are My Wellies? Small steps and giant leaps to green living with style. 2008. p.13

## 8. Inspiring others/Influencing stakeholders/Changing behaviour

59. Robbie Bates, Rebecca Ford and Josie Warden. Space to Regenerate. RSA Journal. Issue 1. 2020
60. https://www.environment.admin.cam.ac.uk/facts-figures#lighting
61. https://www.environment.admin.cam.ac.uk/facts-figures#lighting

## 9. Recycling

62. Anna Shepard. How Green Are My Wellies? Small steps and giant leaps to green living with style. 2008. p.27
63. https://www.environment.admin.cam.ac.uk/facts-figures#lighting.
64. https://www.environment.admin.cam.ac.uk/facts-figures#lighting.

## 10. Think

65. Terry Pratchett. Johnny and the Dead. 1993

## Let's wrap up

66. Dr Katherine Hayhoe. Here's how your climate-related choices are contagious (in a good way!). https://ideas.ted.com/seeing-climate-change-solutions-inspires-collective-action-book-excerpt. Accessed October 2021
67. Terry Pratchett. The Shepherd's Crown. 2015

# References

## Books

Brophy, Sarah S., and Wylie, Elizabeth. The Green Museum. A Primer on Environmental Practice, Second Edition. 2013.

Ki Culture. Energy. A Step-by-Step Guide for Sustainable Action. Vol 1. January 2021.

Shepard, Anna. How Green Are My Wellies? Small steps and giant leaps to green living with style. 2008.

The 1.5ºC Business Playbook. 2021. https://exponentialroadmap.org/1-5c-business-playbook/

## Articles

Attenborough, Will. The Equity Pension is Changing for the Greener. https://www.equity.org.uk/news/2021/october/the-equity-pension-is-changing-for-the-greener/?link_id=3&can_id=af29b3f6abeb95c5096e78ccf68519f7&source=email-discrimination-at-work-your-right-to-equal-treatment&email_referrer=email_1325063&email_subject=equitys-pension-scheme-is-changing-for-the-greener-_

Bates, Robbie, Ford, Rebecca and Warden, Josie. Space to Regenerate. RSA Journal. Issue 1. 2020.

Christine Figueres. In Conversation. RSA Journal. Issue 1. 2020.

Hooker, Lucy. Green Investing: How your savings can fight climate change. https://www.bbc.co.uk/news/business-58544966

Kearns, Ian and Kingsley, Peter. Risky Business. RSA Journal. Issue 1. 2020.

Megan de Silva and Jane Henderson. Sustainability in Conservation Practice. Journal of the Institute of Conservation. Volume 34. Number 1. 2011

Rippon, Tom. On Purpose. RSA Journal. Issue 1. 2020.

Wiseman, Lauren. Let's make our workplace sustainable. World Wide Fund for Nature. https://www.wwf.org.uk/updates/top-20-tips-workplaces-sustainable

A Guide to Global Internet Energy Usage. Energy Helpline. https://www.energyhelpline.com/help/a-guide-to-global-internet-energy-usage

Clicking Green. Who is Winning the Race to Build a Green Internet? Greenpeace. 2017. http://www.clickclean.org

Climate Solutions at Work. An Employee Guide to Drawdown Aligned Business. Project Drawdown. September 2021.

Environmental Sustainability in the Digital Age of Culture. Opportunities, Impacts and Emerging Practices. Julie's Bicycle. 2020. https://juliesbicycle.com/category/resource_hub/

Going Green. Equity Newsletter. 24th June 2021.

Green Tips. World Wide Fund for Nature. https://www.worldwildlife.org/pages/green-tips

Greening the Office. Julie's Bicycle. 2015.

Paper and the Environment. Julie's Bicycle. 2015.

Shady Ships. Retail Giants Pollute Communities and Climate with Fossil-Fueled Ocean Shipping. 2021. https://www.pacificenvironment.org/wp-content/uploads/2021/07/SIZ_Shady-Ships-Report.pdf

The Value of Re-using Household Waste Electrical and Electronic Equipment: 2011 www.wrap.org.uk/sites/files/wrap/WRAP%20WEEE%20HWRC%20summary%20report.pdf

Waterwise. https://www.waterwise.org.uk/save-water/

Water Saving Tips. Eden Project. https://www.edenproject.com/learn/eden-at-home/water-saving-tips

## Videos

Climate Solutions 101. Project Drawdown. 2021. https://drawdown.org/climate-solutions-101

Nili Gilbert. The Crucial Intersection of Climate and Capital. TED https://www.ted.com/talks/nili_gilbert_the_crucial_intersection_of_climate_and_capital?language=en

# About the author

Lorraine Finch has been described as a 'hippy tree hugger'. She's these plus an activist, social entrepreneur and accredited conservator. She is founder and director of LFCP, which is accelerating the cultural heritage sector's climate and environmental actions through research, knowledge sharing and resource creation.

Lorraine makes regular podcasts, writes blogs and gives training on preservation, conservation and sustainability.

Printed in Great Britain
by Amazon